Spinning to Mars

Micros

by Meg Pokrass

BLUE LIGHT PRESS ◆ 1ST WORLD PUBLISHING

SAN FRANCISCO ◆ FAIRFIELD ◆ DELHI

Winner of the 2020 Blue Light Book Award

Spinning to Mars

BLUE LIGHT PRESS
www.bluelightpress.com
bluelightpress@aol.com

1ST WORLD PUBLISHING
PO Box 2211
Fairfield, IA 52556
www.1stworldpublishing.com

BOOK & COVER DESIGN
Melanie Gendron
melaniegendron999@gmail.com

AUTHOR PHOTO
Miriam Berkley

FIRST EDITION

Library of Congress Cataloging-in-Publication Data

ISBN: 978-1-4218-3688-1

For S.C.

Acknowledgements

Grateful acknowledgement is made to the following journals, in which many of these pieces first appeared in different forms: *Wigleaf, elimae, Press 53, Vox Populi, New Flash Fiction Review.*

Contents

"To love or to have loved, that is enough. Ask nothing further. There is no other pearl to be found in the dark folds of life."

— Victor Hugo, *Les Misérables*

Ride to Mars

See the red planet in my eyes, Kitten? Dad said, teeth stacked up like snow cones.

"Only vertical trip worth taking."

Sometimes it feels as if he's still sitting around, waiting for the milky world to line up and trust him.

People will fall for anything.

Some dangle the promise of a ride to Mars. Others dangle the promise of *home*.

Lost Marbles

Life was a parade of stories about the stuff her father did. Her unfaithful father, who had left her his marble collection.

Her mother explained how he'd been a wolf. How she would be home working, sweeping with the tall kitchen broom, and he'd wobble in looking like he just won at Russian roulette.

"The man had serious intimacy issues, but he wasn't all bad," she said. "He hugged like a teddy-bear. And oh, that wonderful collection of antique marbles he had!" She used to say this near Christmas.

"They must be here somewhere."

Dry Skin

She would scream on the weekends, throw shoes at her wall. Her father's problems itched like dry skin. She sank a wooden leaf, imagining it was her father, and still it floated.

Later, trouble had something to do with the light in her walk-in closet, the smoke from patchouli incense holding her still. Music tinted the air with who she was, who she had become. Soon, she would be meeting a boy, not her boyfriend, by the creek at midnight. The honeysuckle flowers would have already bloomed, and she would teach the new boy to suck out drops of honey from the stems on the lawn. She would show him how to be that gentle — to get the drop to come out just right.

Lucky

Your mother said you were *starting up again*, like in books and movies. The first thing you understood about escaping to California was this; you would never have snow again.

You'd see it in Christmas movies. Would wave at it in the distance, glinting and winking from the peaks of the Santa Ynes mountains.

There would be Jasmine flowers, Eucalyptus trees, small butterflies. Smells that overwhelm a family with the feeling of "lucky".

Love Street

You wanted to be live on Love Street. To steal paperbacks about salvation sex and hide them under your bed. You told yourself that one day the sound of your name would make a man sick and then well.

You grew up to be a grown-up who got smoked out by previous lovers after sneaking their animals into your life. The dog was your very first love. You were criminal friends. She'd sneak the cat's food and you'd let her do it.

What did you plan to do with your life? Escape normalcy. Find a man with a dog and a walk-in closet and make yourself sick and then well. Feel better when smoking a man's calmness.

Boy Music

You're fifteen and a boy is coming over. He bounces like music but looks like a human frog, all buggy-eyed and bubble-cheeked. You're not sure why you want to touch him. On the way to school he walks beside you, careful not to interrupt your gait. You let him kiss you on the mouth. He lives near the racetrack, waits like a shadow. *We're too young for anything*, you say. You kiss each other's faces, but the melody comes later, behind the cafeteria.

Moments with Crochet Hooks

Back then she and her mother waited for the phone to ring, for money to plump itself up and walk through their door. Moments passed with yarn and crochet hooks.

She made hats that never fit, put them away in a trunk with games they didn't play. She twirled her hair like twine. Her mother sat alone on Saturdays, yelled at politicians on television.

She dreamt about kissing the bubble-cheeked boys who ran around the playing field.

Wave Riders

The thrill of pony rides, the quiet of a tourist park in October. The feeling that her father was looking at her, but she couldn't remember his face.

Growing up on the warm beaches, her belly button was open to the world like an eye, watching for trouble. Boys were called, "Conch" and "Bong". They rode waves, and she watched them.

Night Heron

She spied him on the platform standing flamingo-like, one clog on the ground, stretching his quadriceps. It seemed the air around him was moving toward a decision. His outer layer was shiny and black. Shards of memory hung from his face.

She was splendid back then, her heart soft as a persimmon. He spied her too, right as the train was curling into the station. She tried to work the odds, to fish for her gloves while making her way closer.

Since then, she's felt bug-bitten and small. He was shorter than her, with a Night Heron slouch. Gelled-up feathers nobody has ever been able to identify.

Custodial

You recall the dreams in which he came back to you. The cracked leather diner seat poking into your thigh when he told you he was leaving you his Christmas cactus. How the plant was going to need a safe home.

You worried about killing it. Said *I don't know how to take care of things*. Still, you watered his plant, learned to admire the gaudy red flower.

"Talk to it," he said. "But never analyze it."

Hitting Back

Her mother, saltier than anyone else's mother, sitting on the toilet seat, door ajar, talking freely about how she had never been loved. How her father, in the early days of their courtship, had probably been the closest call.

She imagined her father slumped over a steering wheel, daylight squinting through his t-shirt, white hairs on his arms like dead grass.

One day she'd see him in a different world perhaps, and she'd ask him about it — about this accident, and the others. Maybe he'd been driving in the middle of the night, struck a moose. Nobody had let them know any of the details, they were too far removed from his life. But she'd heard of people hitting animals and animals, in the throes of death, hitting back.

Light as Fluff

Once, you came across a story in the paper about a child who followed her father into the Siberian wilds. Two weeks later, with her arms cut to shreds, someone found her alive.

The good Samaritan interviewed described her as "a miracle". "Light as fluff, hardly there". Picked her up and carried her to a better place.

Hammertoe

Now you awake with your mother's hammertoe. In this tightness you have become her. How often she told you it hurt. You never knew exactly what to say.

You do not know how to comfort yourself since she died, so you complain about your hammertoe to anyone who will listen. This is how you commune with your mother, who lives in your little toe.

Hips

In young adulthood, men liked your hips. Thought they looked capable of pushing a good baby out.

As predicted, he popped out right on time, no drugs necessary.

"Man that baby's swarthy!" a nurse chirped.

A few random husbands followed, smiling their way up through family photos, poking their heads out of the past.

Lasso

Driving from station to station, her customers were gas station managers. She sold them advertising enhanced cash register tape. Stuff most customers threw out.

Her eyes grew tired, so she practiced in her mirror. The trick was to position the tape around a station owner's shoulders like a lasso. To get them laughing, touching it, eager for whatever came next.

Back at her office she'd add up her numbers, snap off the ends of her hair.

Times Square, 1989

You sang songs nobody wanted to hear. Flew through the starry city full of GIRLS, GIRLS, GIRLS! Central Park wildings, muggers, cabdrivers with parakeets. A tube of lipstick in your fist like blood or prayer. The Kiss Me Red pointing to your clamshell mouth.

You were not yet stuck, not really. The men had names like Guy and Tom, but none of the names fit them. Their penises shrank and grew like mushrooms or flowers. You felt sorry for all of them, in your greedy young way.

Your hips swayed through Riverside park, uncurling your face to the sun. This was the clockwise track they all smile about. Even hamsters smile.

Teeth

Heart pumping against your back, he said he wanted to be with you forever as though you would want to know it, but you could barely hear him over the barking of a dog down the block, some confused or tired dog. You still loved him then because he would nod his head at sounds as though he really heard them. He'd laugh as if your thoughts were just right for him.

Kissing, you'd keep your eyes open, lips shut. Those awful teeth you had in middle school, the ones they corrected too late — you felt them there every time. It was them being kissed. Not you.

Dial Up

The dial up preacher said it this way:
Love is similar to the voice of God.
A very, very, very special fruit.
Each "very" he said softer than the one before it.
"Fruit" was whispered.

Perhaps his words were sliding-scale based.
He had more audible things to say
for those who upgraded
from "White Rose Basic Vows".

Fires

You found yourself singing about the fires at home. How your husband made fires and how you warmed your hands, embracing the heatwave.

New Year's Day Photograph

The one sitting next to you at your mother's dining room table was in love with you. Silently you thought of him as *cute but dumb*.

"Not smart enough for you," your mother confirmed this after winning ten games of Scrabble against him, tallying the score. But the two of you looked so happy in this New Year's Day photo, leaning into your glasses of champagne, smiling at your mother.

Mugged

When the man stepped out from behind the wall and grabbed you hard, you smiled because you didn't understand. But when he walked away and left you bleeding — you had a new plan.

The first thing you did: You fell in love.
The second thing: You adopted two old cats.

Mountain Gorillas

He was your perennial sidekick. Called you his 'mountain gorilla'. You'd make silly grunting noises to each other over yogurt in the morning. Would wake up like tired middle-aged zombies after eating too much Chinese takeaway. Meet in the kitchen and laugh about how awful both of you looked with MSG pockets underneath your eyes. "Fancy meeting you here, Bonzo," you'd both say.

Between Animals

He lay next to her on the bed, facing the wall. It had become his sleepy-time signal, the message was to leave him alone, that sex wasn't even a remote possibility. She reminded him that he once referred to her as a 'pet replacement'. How a long while ago, he'd shown her photos of his lost cat, he had hundreds of them from the time the cat was a speck of white kitten.

"Do you think that this might be part of the problem with us?" she said.

She imagined climbing the Everest of his body, perching on the top of his belly like a sexy squid, dangling her breasts like fishing lines. He was still in love with that cat. She shouldn't have let her hair come in white.

Unreliable Map

She and her husband were moving to a larger place, big enough for a baby or two. *Big enough for anything*, he said. Loping across her front lawn, she glanced up at the sky; ginger clouds with unknowable footprints, like a map she could follow if she only trusted. Every one of them seemed to be pointing somewhere else.

Traffic

When the cars did start to move, she began to remember how beautiful living near the ocean was. She remembered that her hair was growing back in and that friends said it looked good on her. She remembered that he could make a healthy dessert parfait, and that she liked it — even though it was loaded with stinky fish oil. All of the good things in the world, when the cars moved, and the sun crept back into her face.

Wonderful Cats

They rescued the two middle-aged cat brothers from the pound. *Yay*, and the brothers warmed up the dining room, colored the windows.

The infection in their hearts worked like a miner's headlamp back then, showed them things and ideas, such as *save some old cats* — and then, the light turned the other way.

You know how confusion paralyses one's best instincts, works by dismembering what is barely there.

A man, a woman, a tattered house, many wonderful cats.

Rupture

She is feeling sorry for herself when the earthquake begins and her house starts to wobble. Hard to calculate the strength of such a rupture. Everything falls and the house sort of cracks. Nobody calls, but the phone rings.

Sister, she says. It is two o-clock. The cat skitters off somewhere and nobody is upset yet there is so much wrong.

Trophies

She stands from bed and floats through the house full of junk.
"This and this and this," is what she thinks, padding past the boxes
of her husband's bowling trophies loved by yellowed newspaper.
She begins to plan her escape in the middle of the night, when
the dollar-shop curtains are drawn, her husband snoring like a
police vehicle.

Time

In the bungalow he owns she sits and watches the clock. Not to complicate — she knits, bakes cornbread, dances away the ice inside her fingers. Once, she carved his name into the shy part of a potato. Back then there was a cat, sand, and a beach.

Normalcy

Your husband was chatting with his girlfriend again. The girlfriend was a geriatric nurse, and so was her sister, he said. How normal, how stupidly normal her family is, you thought. But this is what he'd always wanted. A practical woman and all the trimmings.

These days, the nurse's expression of contempt hung on the walls of your mind like a colorless photograph.

The trick was sitting on the beach very close to the water, but not so close it would cover your head. Trying to imagine how bad her sense of humor might be.

Efficiency

Your next lover; an efficiency expert, hooks a paw around your shoulders. *I really do love you* he says. Has loved you ever since he saw your cute smile in the *Married But Miserable* Facebook group.

This reminds you of the time you almost adopted a middle-aged cat. You saw her on the internet and you loved her too much, but she was an animal with many complications.

"Why didn't I meet you twenty years ago?" he says. You smile at the promise of his downturned lips. You're tired, and you miss your husband, but you let his lips cover your body in fishy nibbles.

Weather

Bad, horrible, of course. Well, it always is, this time of year. That sucks. Really, I'm used to it. Right. Sure, it is depressing, but it really doesn't get to me. I'm glad to hear it. Okay, it's hard, but you get used to it. So true, we do get used to our lives, whatever they are. Well, not really, I mean it is impossible to not wish for better. True. What do you wish for? I wish for something better.

Bond Villain You

In this photo, younger you with the look a James Bond movie villain. Eyes murderous. She glares at you angrily, upper lip curling.

Extends her unwrinkled neck.

Strangles your sad old mouth with her perfect young lips. Can't feel sad about anything that has happened.

Soup

In a house in the middle of nowhere, serenity was a can of soup. The air just full of waiting. She preferred his brown coffee mugs — the ones that felt strong. She knew he would cook for her — would drive up and be able to park and say things men say.

Things like, "A broken house doesn't matter, I can fix it."

Just the thought of it made her twirl. She'd bang up against the windows, blind to glass.

Let's Say

Let's say you meet again the next day, after watching each other's best scenes at home. You sit on a bench near a duck pond and kiss without touching "send".

You slide a hand through his hair, smile at his warm eyes and tell him which one of his movies you love the most: it's the one about the gorilla who is so lonely he can't stop masturbating. He tells you which one of your movies he loves, the one about the rebellious teenager. "I'll bet you were just like her," he says. He tells you that he could probably fall in love with your childhood.

Dream of the Cat

You were slouching in your bedroom alone again, an adult person, mother and wife, thinking of how the hills seemed shadowed in front, but lit from behind. Why was it that way and not the other?

Trying not to blink; feeling the cat still there in the house — trapped.

It might have had something do with the dream of a dying cat who had never really died. How the cat dreams kept getting stronger as the house grew weaker.

Modalities

One night he brought home sinus medicine from the pharmacy — the wrong kind again, but he insisted she try it because it cost money.

"Just lie still," he said. He squeezed the cone to her nose. "Snort!"

She followed orders. That was one thing she knew how to do. Her head was thunder, water flew out like trust.

Cursed Night

You remember when you turned sixteen and there was a bubbling as though a tightly filled creek had reached the edge. You were full of anger and swallowed it down. You'd dance with a man naked if he would take you inside his house and listen. You believed it was time to dance with the cursed night. You were never afraid of hell. Only of being a girl in a house full of so many turned-off lights.

Doctor Love

One might surmise that she never wanted to get better because she'd lose him. Needed to see him peek around the corner of the exam room, holding her huge, thick chart over his heart, covering his eyes from the years of notes. Sliding his fingers away from his eyes, widening them with a grin, saying, "Here we are, looking so young, I can't quite remember, have we turned thirty yet?"

Trying to make her laugh at the start of each visit. Pain bringing its own bench.

Separation

Your husband is reading on the bed. After packing your third bag, you find yourself staring at his penis which pokes out the side of his shorts when he lies down. It has always been friendly. You're going to miss it. "You're staring," he says. Your stomach is rotted out from too much coffee. He rolls out of bed, grabs a Kleenex box on the bookcase. His mollusk mouth closed and round.

Two miscarriages in two years. Each time you adopted an adult cat. One of them, the tiger cat, dozing on the foot of the bed. "Remove this animal," he says.

You pick her up and take her to the sunny living room. On the bed, when you come back in, his shorts are off, not his shirt. His right hand is already moving evenly, tenderly. He seems to want you to watch, is gazing at you with a tiny smile, so you unbutton your shirt. His sperm is rising — hopeful and stupid. The room smells like fresh bread.

Conclusive

They fought again that night, but this time it was conclusive. Right there in the room — the smell of some younger animal trying to get in. And, although they were bending toward unpleasant words, a forgiving shadow appeared between them sometimes.

Movies

At movies, she cried during all the parts that no one else remembered. To cry at all, in a movie, is scrunching up in the corner of your life and seeing what is sad, or good, but wrong, or *what could have been*.

She cried inwardly, so maybe 'crying' was not the right word for what she did — the correct word would not please her, anyway. She didn't feel alone when alone, but sometimes she felt so next to others.

Blue Heron

At the airport you met up with his Great Blue Heron. It had been slouching near a nasty spill of chili-fries in the first-floor cafe. This was the cafe where he'd left you (and the bird) with a two-hour wait before boarding the plane.

His ex was at the hospital and his phone kept ringing. He buzzed and rang and limped through the airport as though hobbled by sound.

She'll never stop trying to win him back, will she? You said to the tall, disoriented bird.

Junkie

Forty years old and espresso is what you live for. You wake up
and drive to the coffee shop. Stand in line like a mid-life junkie.
Shrink when anyone says hello, pull up your hoodie.

You're a middle-aged juvenile delinquent, you tell yourself
grinning inside your soul, amusing yourself to no end.

The husband and you were a great comedy team, until he stopped
laughing. Now you're a coffee-addicted person who can still ruin
men's lives just by staying so funny and young-spirited.

Moosewick

When she moved in with Bob, she found out how quiet a human could be. There was just this nothingness between them over a dish of strawberries.

Bob and his shiny eyes fixated on the dogs. *I sure love these pups*, you'd say, trying to loosen the conversation, to kick up an echo. He'd stare at his fork.

This kept her losing weight, not a bad outcome entirely. She was half the woman she used to be. Hard to find her own squeaky voice, so she took to visiting another man in dreams. She'd call him 'Moosewick', this moose of a man who sang as if he'd reinvented the Broadway musical. Who talked so much her ears became embroidered.

Feverish

Even now, in dreams, the diluted tortoiseshell claims your bed,
the cats taking shifts. In the morning, you crave the white one
feverishly, her smell, her girth. Tequila helps. The feeling of it
padding down the hallway of your throat.

Mute Fantasies

"It's not in your nature to say these things," she said, feeling color rush back into her face. He said he loved her too much. That when he left in the morning (when he moved away for good) he'd become old.

In the end, they agreed on one thing:

That being married to someone else had made him capable of loving her again.

"We're finally here," he said.

Unexpected Wisdom on the Phone

There is only one person who cheers her up. She calls him at bedtime. He always surprises her with the random thoughts he has. "Puritans had the greatest sex," he says. It almost sounds true.

Dream of Dying

You're attached to an oxygen supply and the prettiest, nicest nurse is called Gina. You would have liked to have had her face, her wonderful breath, her tenderness. Her luck in love.

You remember the smell of your father's cigarette breath, the freedom he felt while sucking on rocket fire.

You're blasting off.

Rust

You thought about the pigeon-colored vase he'd given you on your fifteenth anniversary. It has been sitting in the yard since the big cat died. You'd cut your last flowers during the time the cat began failing, the world's best cat, there was no other and never would be — and you couldn't bring the vase inside anymore. *Let it rust,* you thought. This is how things were with the two of you now. This was why you stopped worrying about any of it.

Classified

She wanted to take one of the saddest men on earth and make him less sad. At a house in the foothills, the sad man from the classified advertisement offered to make her lunch.

"Please don't worry," she said when his dog stuck his nose into her crotch. He was annoyed with his dog, kept saying "Down! Down!" which made the dog more amorous.

A smile obscured his sadness. His belly poked out of his shirt and he pushed it back with his hand.

She knelt and smoothed the dog's ears. The dog had rancid breath and she liked it.

Anticipation

When he brings over the donuts, they'll gawk at the them and sniff them inside the box for an hour before taking a bite.

The shape of lust is round, the solid feeling that a person isn't the same flavor every day, even if they are. Some days the glaze is thicker.

This one is for you, he'll say, *because it reminds me of your smile.*

Newness

There were butterscotch people and she had never been one of them. Any portrait of her would be blurry, you'd probably not know what to think. She got in the shower hoping for newness.

They were still at the beginning. A coveted, lovely place to be. Curtains were open, the sky welcomed rain. Someday they'd toast to how carefully they had navigated it all.

Optimists

"No," she said to him, "I'm tired, and sick of it too." She pulled in her hips.

"Well okay then!" he said.

Nothing worked with her these days, so he shrugged and started pulling at his beard. Wasn't it Winston Churchill who said that optimists preferred to sleep with pessimists?

Silent Types

"Silent types," she said to soothe herself. She said this to herself to make up for the faults of men who could not talk to her about the baggage of having feelings.

She was something of a spunky animation called "woman confused". Her words were imprisoned in a grape-shaped dialog bubble. It echoed as she walked her fat dog to the bottom of the hill so it could sniff around leaner dogs and their spunky, married owners. She had a bit of husband-envy, which was not at all sinister. Just sad.

She wanted to wrap her paws around another dog's face, to leap on another creature and be pushed back on the gritty floor. To inhale the bouillon breath of beast-love upon her.

The Ghost of Christmas Past

The tinsel of his texts. The sparkle. For twelve days before, every night, bludgeoning the Christmas blues. Has it been ten years? And we're back again, two puddles of weary. "Happy frankincense and myrrh, happy almost Christmas to you, don't give up on me," he wrote. "I never have," you write. You've loved him since you began stealing raw cookie dough from the bowl. You must have been eighteen years old, wearing polyester sweaters, always needing a male this unreliable. This drained.

Old Girls

Wind in your faces, the two of you drove to the warmest part of the coast. It was beautiful there, the hills smooth and set wide. And the wind felt so warm, so right for it.

"Put a bra on those mountains!" you hooted. Here you were, running away like kids together. Laughing about mountains that looked like breasts, even though both of yours were gone.

Cat Displacement

The cat would snuggle into his neck. I would snuggle in and displace the cat. Would hold him and the cat, and forget about the world outside of his tiny, musty room. I hid beneath his comforter. When morning came, I could barely tell where I was. A continent away I remembered my doctor and that I had ruined my marriage. And sometimes I forgot.

Slanted Variation

Her hands flutter over her features, run to hide in the bathroom, hoping they'll stop trying to smooth themselves out. She looks in the mirror, smelling the scent of piss from so many train-sad ladies. She's her own slanted variation, a crazy-assed mail-order bride, the kind of human she's never wanted to be. And yet she's landed, plonk! Staccato-slumped, tone-deaf, right there in his station.

Giant and Duck

On the scrim of your brain the ocean inches forward; threaten-
ing sandcastles, flattening faces. Your freckles pop out like sighs.
Sand crabs shush each other in a labyrinth of crooked tunnels
underneath matching towels. This day you make up stories: You're
a giant, he's a duck. You both laugh at the way it appears.

Intact

He had been gone for so long. What is there to say? You wanted to say so many things to him but the words had long ago died. *You're really alive?* you said.

I think so, he said.

You were on a video call. His virtual background looked dusty and red, as if he was calling from Mars.

He held up his long human fingers to show you how many he had. Nothing appeared to be missing.

Bingo

When the woman was young, she fell for a clown called Bingo. She thought he probably loved her back. His trained mime's fingers made her feel friendly. Her toes made the clown happy too.

But sometimes he'd bite.

"Love bites," he'd call them. It would hurt like hell, and she'd cry, but she let him know how much she needed those wounds. How he reminded her of her father, who died when she was five. *It doesn't really hurt*, she'd say.

Short, Happy Movie

This kind of thing is not unmovable, he said. He lay on the futon, knees curled ike a question mark. He was not ready to leave, and she wanted nothing more than to love him again. But if he stayed, the distrust would win.

"We're all just beams from a lightless star," he said. "Stop trying so hard."

And then he was moving away from her bed, over to his floor mat, stretching his dancing legs — readying to fly.

Winter Garden

Working in her winter garden was like deciding which patches of life were worth keeping. Bright sky days, she'd sing to the feral cats. She was harming nothing. Weeds kill everything eventually. Friends who disapproved of her choices had already grown distant. They lived in healthier climates. Tended gardens with direct sunlight.

Home

You took long walks and let your mind dance stupidly. The holidays would be the worst part, no turning away from it. Your marriage over, your mother had died. You reminded yourself that you had a new land, a part-time lover, and the Atlantic was as still as a lake.

For the first time since you were little, you could see your breath in winter. Could point to it and say *there it is*.

For the rest of your life you'd find sneaky ways to feed the memories that scratched on your door, trying to get in.

Greetings

They say otters don't live here anymore, but they certainly seem to visit. You saw one lying on its back, nearly a cripple, licking its foot the day the new neighbor moved in. He looked as if he'd just been on safari. Or like someone's missing father, carting bags of crap into an empty apartment.

You were hoping for some shut eye, and maybe a neighbor who was just a bit less hinky, but *you get what you get.*

Dear me, you said, and he smiled a loopy smile right at you. You could tell he thought you were coming on to him. Men always thought so about you, even though you were nearly a half- century old. You both stood there, staring at the depressed looking otter.

"That thing looks dead," you said. "But he's come here to greet you."

Truce

They sit outside at the summer cafe, whole lobsters on plates in front of them. He smiles a worried, old man smile. A smile she's come to know from photographs.

"You're as pretty as I thought you'd be," he says. "You look just like your mother, only kinder around the eyes."

"I've brought you something," she says and hands her father a paperweight. A clear block of amber with an ancient cockroach stuck inside it.

"Interesting," he says.

"What else would you expect from your kid?"

The question will always remain encrusted between them: Why did he leave on her fifth birthday, right as she was learning to fly?

They set about trying to look fearless, pulling their lobsters apart. "You're better than me with these prickly things," he says, not smiling.

She tears the legs from their lobsters, breaks them in half, watches his face while she pries out the meat. Raises a severed leg to the sky.

About the Author

Meg Pokrass is the author of seven flash fiction collections, including "Damn Sure Right" (Press 53, 2011), "The Dog Looks Happy Upside Down" (Etruscan Press, 2016), "The Dog Seated Next to Me", (Pelekinesis, 2019), "Cellulose Pajamas" (Blue Light Book Award, 2016), the chapbooks "An Object At Rest" (Ravenna Press, 2020) and "Alice in Wonderland Syndrome" (V. Press, 2020) and two novellas-in-flash: "Here, Where We Live" (Rose Metal Press, 2014) and "The Loss Detector" (Bamboo Dart Press, 2020). Meg's flash fiction, prose poetry and hybrid writing has been widely internationally anthologized; in *New Micro: Exceptionally Short Fiction* (W.W. Norton & Co., 2018) *and Flash Fiction International* (W.W. Norton & Co., 2015), *The Best Small Fictions (2018 & 2019),* the *Wigleaf Top 50, The Best Irish and British Flash Fiction Award,* as well as many other anthologies. Her work has appeared in *Electric Literature, Waxwing, Washington Square Review, Tin House, Smokelong, McSweeney's, Wigleaf, MoonPark Review, Five Points, Hobart Pulp, Split Lip,* and over the last decade, nearly one-thousand literary journals. Meg serves as Founding Co-Editor of the Best Microfiction anthology series and Festival Curator for Flash Fiction Festival, U.K.

CPSIA information can be obtained
at www.ICGtesting.com
Printed in the USA
BVHW031039230621
610210BV00007B/713